Lions

Victoria Blakemore

vblakemore.author@gmail.com

Copyright info/picture credits

Cover, Maggy Meyer/AdobeStock; Page 3, tpsdave/Pixabay; Page 5, Pexels/Pixabay; Page 7, kdsphotos/Pixabay; Page 9, Maciej Czekajewski/Adobestock; Pages 10-11, Iuliia Sokolovska/AdobeStock; Page 13, Pexels/Pixabay; Page 15, OlaEklund/Pixabay; Page 17, HowardWilks/Pixabay; Page 19, Graham-H/Pixabay; Page 21, Pexels/Pixabay; Page 23; eter-itlux/Pixabay; Page 25, NicholasDeloitteMedia/Pixabay; Page 27, DaFranzos/Pixabay; Page 29, Andrea Izzotti/AdobeStock; Page 31, Pexels/Pixabay; Page 33, Maggy Meyer/AdobeStock

Table of Contents

What Are Lions?

Lions are large mammals. They are members of the cat family. Other members of the cat family include tigers, leopards, and jaguars.

Lions are one of the largest of the big cats. The only cat that is larger than a lion is a tiger.

Lions have fur that is yellow and tan. This helps them to blend in with the grasses of their habitat.

Size

Lions can be between five and nine feet long. Females can weigh up to about 400 pounds. Males can weigh up to about 600 pounds.

Female lions are smaller then males. This makes them faster and better at hunting.

Physical Characteristics

Lions have sharp claws and teeth. This helps them to catch their prey when they are hunting.

A lion's claws are **retractable**. They are hidden until the lion needs them to come out. This prevents the claws from getting in the way of running.

Male lions have a thick mane of hair around their neck. This helps to protect them when they are fighting with other male lions.

Habitat

Lions are found in the savannas and woodlands. The long grasses of their habitat make it easier for them to sneak up on their prey.

It can be very dry where lions live. They have to get much of their water from the food they eat.

Range

Most lions are found in parts of central and southern Africa.

They can also be found in

some parts of India.

Diet

Lions are **carnivores**. This means that they eat only meat.

Their diet is made up of mammals such as antelope, zebra, buffalo, and wildebeest.

Lions also **scavenge** prey that has been caught by other predators.

Lions are ambush hunters.
They sneak up on their prey,
then pounce. They
sometimes hunt in small
groups so they can surround
their prey.

Most of their hunting is done
at night when it is easiest to
sneak up on prey.

The lionesses do most of the
hunting. They bring food back
to the other lions.

Communication

Lions use scent, sound, and movement to communicate. They may show their teeth as a warning. They also mark their **territory** with a special scent that tells other lions to stay away.

Lions may roar, grunt, snarl, or puff to communicate.

A lion's roar is very loud. It can

be heard from miles away.

Movement

Lions can run very fast when they are hunting. They have been recorded running as fast as fifty miles per hour.

They are only able to run this fast for short distances. They need to be close to their prey when they start running.

Lions are able to climb trees.

They are sometimes seen

resting on tree branches.

Pride Life

Lions live in large groups that are called prides. A pride can be made up of up to thirty lions.

Prides work together to hunt, protect their territory, and take care of cubs. They also spend much of their time sleeping.

Male lions sometimes fight

each other for control of the

pride.

Lion Cubs

Lions usually have a litter of up to four babies, or cubs. The pride works together to take care of cubs.

Male cubs usually leave when they are about two years old. Females usually stay with their mother in the pride.

When cubs are born, they have dark spots on their fur. These spots disappear as cubs get older.

Lifespan

In the wild, lions often live between ten and fourteen years. In **captivity**, they may live as long as twenty years.

Lions live longer in captivity because there is always food available. They are also safe from habitat destruction and hunting.

Lionesses usually live longer than male lions. This is because male lions often fight over territory.

Population

Most lions are listed as **vulnerable**. If their population keeps **declining**, they could soon be **endangered**.

There are thought to be around 20,000 lions in the wild. There are over 1,000 in zoos around the world.

There are thought to be

between 300 and 500 lions

left in India.

Circus Lions

Lions have been used in circus acts for many years. The circuses travel and entertain people in lots of different places.

Some people think that lions should not be made to perform in circuses. They think lions should be free.

Many circuses have stopped

using lions. The lions are

released into special **preserves**.

Helping Lions

There are many different **conservation** groups that are working to help lions.

Some groups focus on the threat of habitat loss. They want to protect lion habitats so lions have a safe place to live.

Other groups are trying to prevent lions from being hunted. They are working to get lions protected by law.

Some researchers study lions and use what they learn to educate others. They believe that people may want to help if they know about the problems lions face.

Glossary

Carnivore: an animal that eats only meat

Captivity: animals that are kept by humans, not in the wild

Conservation: the act of keeping safe from loss and destruction

Declining: getting smaller

Endangered: at risk of becoming extinct

Preserves: special areas of land set up to protect plants and animals

Retractable: able to be pulled back in

Scavenge: to eat leftovers that other animals leave behind after hunting

Territory: an area of land that an animal claims as its own

Vulnerable: an animal that is likely to become endangered

About the Author

Victoria Blakemore is a first grade

teacher in Southwest Florida with a

passion for reading.

You can visit her at

www.elementaryexplorers.com

Also in This Series

Elementary Explorers **Gray Wolves** Victoria Blakemore	Elementary Explorers **Sloths** Victoria Blakemore	Elementary Explorers **Flamingos** Victoria Blakemore	Elementary Explorers **Camels** Victoria Blakemore	Elementary Explorers **Koalas** Victoria Blakemore	Elementary Explorers **Honey Bees** Victoria Blakemore
Elementary Explorers **Pandas** Victoria Blakemore	Elementary Explorers **Pangolins** Victoria Blakemore	Elementary Explorers **White-Tailed Deer** Victoria Blakemore	Elementary Explorers **Orcas** Victoria Blakemore	Elementary Explorers **Giraffes** Victoria Blakemore	Elementary Explorers **Corn** Victoria Blakemore
Elementary Explorers **Meerkats** Victoria Blakemore	Elementary Explorers **Echidnas** Victoria Blakemore	Elementary Explorers **Walruses** Victoria Blakemore	Elementary Explorers **Raccoons** Victoria Blakemore	Elementary Explorers **Bald Eagles** Victoria Blakemore	Elementary Explorers **Apples** Victoria Blakemore
Elementary Explorers **Arctic Foxes** Victoria Blakemore	Elementary Explorers **Red Pandas** Victoria Blakemore	Elementary Explorers **Cassowaries** Victoria Blakemore	Elementary Explorers **Tigers** Victoria Blakemore	Elementary Explorers **Ladybugs** Victoria Blakemore	Elementary Explorers **Moose** Victoria Blakemore
Elementary Explorers **Beluga Whales** Victoria Blakemore	Elementary Explorers **Leopards** Victoria Blakemore	Elementary Explorers **Elephants** Victoria Blakemore	Elementary Explorers **Jellyfish** Victoria Blakemore	Elementary Explorers **Binturongs** Victoria Blakemore	Elementary Explorers **Lions** Victoria Blakemore
Elementary Explorers **Dolphins** Victoria Blakemore	Elementary Explorers **Reindeer** Victoria Blakemore	Elementary Explorers **Hammerhead Sharks** Victoria Blakemore	Elementary Explorers **Hippos** Victoria Blakemore	Elementary Explorers **Pumpkins** Victoria Blakemore	Elementary Explorers **Peafowl** Victoria Blakemore

Also in This Series

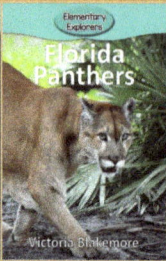

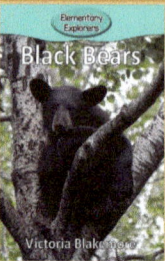

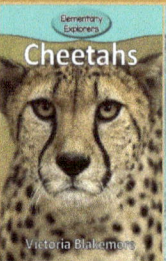

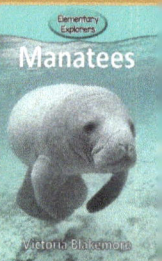

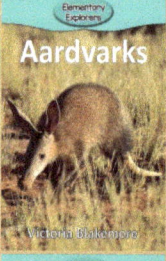

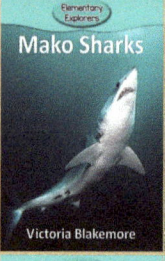

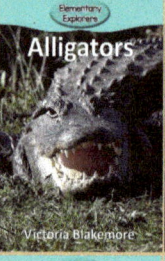

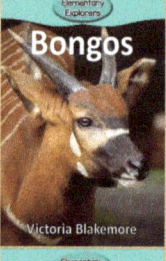

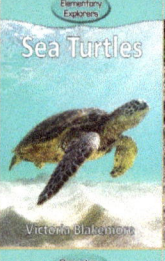

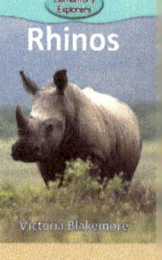

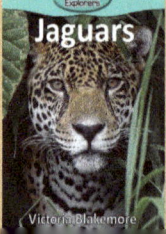

Chameleons — Victoria Blakemore

Florida Panthers — Victoria Blakemore

Aye-Ayes — Victoria Blakemore

Black Bears — Victoria Blakemore

Cheetahs — Victoria Blakemore

Manatees — Victoria Blakemore

Gingerbread — Victoria Blakemore

Polar Bears — Victoria Blakemore

Hot Chocolate — Victoria Blakemore

Orangutans — Victoria Blakemore

Coyotes — Victoria Blakemore

Marshmallows — Victoria Blakemore

Strawberries — Victoria Blakemore

Aardvarks — Victoria Blakemore

Mako Sharks — Victoria Blakemore

Alligators — Victoria Blakemore

Frogs — Victoria Blakemore

Hedgehogs — Victoria Blakemore

Brown Bears — Victoria Blakemore

Bongos — Victoria Blakemore

Sea Turtles — Victoria Blakemore

Quokkas — Victoria Blakemore

Muskrats — Victoria Blakemore

Zebras — Victoria Blakemore

Red Foxes — Victoria Blakemore

Ring-Tailed Lemurs — Victoria Blakemore

Platypuses — Victoria Blakemore

Anteaters — Victoria Blakemore

Kangaroos — Victoria Blakemore

Rhinos — Victoria Blakemore

Jaguars — Victoria Blakemore

Wombats — Victoria Blakemore

www.ingramcontent.com/pod-product-compliance
Lightning Source LLC
Chambersburg PA
CBHW051252020426
42333CB00025B/3175